Define Me, the definition game

Let the language flow and whirl around your head.

Define Me, the definition game

Define Me, the definition game

Content overview

<u>Define Me</u>

Multiplayer Version

The fun definition game with the addicting twist and knack for knowledge

- *suitable for small and not so small groups*
- *improves your English and creativity*
- *increases knowledge and vocabulary*

<u>What you need:</u>

pencils

scrap paper

improvisational skill

creativity

<u>What to prepare</u>

First time: Copy the cards onto cardboard or normal paper with several glued layers and cut them out.

Choose the editions you want to play with or just use all cards, also add the blank cards to even out the number of cards in each players hands.

The available, playable editions are:

- ⊕ Slang, indicated with a S in the lower right hand corner of the card
- ⊕ Medical & Biology, M
- ⊕ Literature, L (also suited for self study of literary terms)
- ⊕ Random and strange, but real words, W

A good number of definitions is 10 per player. Distribute the cards with the definitions and the blank ones among the players evenly. Put the cards with the words to define on a stack upside down. Also hand out enough scrap paper.

How to

At first the players should take a look at their given cards. These are for their eyes only.

The youngest person begins with drawing a card from the words-only-stack and reads it out aloud as well as he/she can.

All players are given a variable amount of time to come up with a convincing definition of the presented word. 2 minutes seem to be enough. You may write your definition down, if so wished.

The aim is to convince others that one's own definition is the right one.

☆ *Idea: To make sure the others do not see that, if so, you have the matching definition card <u>pretend</u> to write one yourself.*

Every player checks his/her cards whether he/she has the matching definition. The one, who does, tries to put it into his/her own words and may alter the definition a bit, so that the others cannot guess right away that the player possesses the matching definition card, but don't change it too much.

That is important for scoring later on.

Then every person reads out their own definition, this will be the most interesting part of the game.

Voting phase

In this phase all players get the chance to present their definitions to the group. The oldest player starts by reading out his definition. The others then follow. After having listened to all definitions, the players get the chance to vote on the different definitions. The scores are given out according to the following table.

Define Me, the definition game

Voting Table

Situation	Points received
Player could trick others with his made-up definition	**+3 for each vote**
Player voted on made-up definition	**-1**
Player voted on right definition	**+1**
Player votes on his own right definition	**-1**
Player votes on own made-up definition	**+1**
Player with right definition and no other vote for it (except for his own)	**+2**
Player with right definition votes for any other made-up definition	**0** *and others receive no points from that player*

Should definitions sound similar the scoring above applies and is divided by 2.

End of the game

The game ends when all words to define are used up.

The player with the highest scores wins.

Scores	Rank
-0	Word Nibbler
0-10	Babbling Blaster
10-20	Word Fool
20-30	Scribe
30-40	Learned Wordzard
40- above	The Real Deal

<u>Define Me</u>

2-Player-Version

This version is for 2 players only taking turns and differs from the multiplayer version in the following rules:

- only use the cards with the definitions on them
- choose a variable amount of cards and distribute them among each other
- one player picks a word from his cards and has to come up with 3 fake definitions her/himself, which the player may write down
- then he/she presents the word and the 4 definitions, the real one plus the 3 fake ones, to the other player, who has to find the right definition
- the points are given out according to the table on the next page

Situation	Points
Player guesses right definition	+1
Player could trick the other one with his made-up definition	+0,5
Player voted on made-up definition	-0,25
Player got 3 definitions right in a row	+2

- as an optional rule for beginners these jokers can be given to each player at the beginning of the game
    - 1 whobble, which enables the player to skip the current word and remove it from the game
    - 3 whibbles, which can be used to delete one of the fake definitions

Define Me, the definition game

Remarks

The game can provide you with a lot of fun at many different occasions. It is the party game to play with your <u>whodis</u>, as well as the <u>mondo</u> good game for school. It might make sense to scale the size of the pages up if you copy them. Cardboard or even laminated cardboard will make the game cards more durable to ensure a longer lifetime.

Despite the ample number of cards, you might run out of fresh words to define. In that case you have 2 possibilities. The first one is to wait until I publish more versions to play with; the second one is to find words yourself. You will find blank pages in this book to write your own new words on. Should you get some inspiration about new categories right now; just write them down on the opposite site.

One last hint: Try not to impress your friends too much with your newly gained knowledge of words. You don 't want to be an antwacky airhead, do you?

-DTT, 2009

Personal Notes:

all to pot	all to pot	S
	messed up	
almond rocks	almond rocks	S
	socks	
amber nectar	amber nectar	S
	Lager, beer	
ankle biters	ankle biters	S
	crawling babies, small children	

antwacky	antwacky	S
	old fashioned	
badload	badload	S
	a drunk person	
Baldwin	Balwin	S
	attractive male	
ballistic therapy	ballistic therapy	S
	being shot	

balloon knot	the rectum	balloon knot	S
coffin nail	cigarette	coffin nail	S
barking spider	imaginary being to blame for farts	barking spider	S
do the Technicolor yawn	to vomit	do the Technicolor yawn	S
buffoon	a stupid person	buffoon	S
dossy	easy	dossy	S
cancer stick	cigarette	cigarette	S
durge	an annyoing person	durge	S
		cancer stick	S

ego surf	ego surf / to look for your own name on the internet	s
froyo	froyo / frozen yogurt	s
get a five finger discount	five finger discount / to steal	s
green apple nasties	diarrhoea	s
	green apple nasties	s
gtg	gtg / got to go	s
get medieval	get medieval / to beat or attack	s
hayseed	hayseed / person from a rural area	s
hug the throne	to vomit	s
	hug the throne	s

hungarian	hungarian	hungry; citizen of Hungary	S
karena	karena	pretty girl	S
kinderkid	kinderkid	wannabee, fake	S
limou	limou	a limousine; shoes	S
mondo	mondo	really, very, extremely / no, negative	S
negatory	negatory	no, negative	S
Omega Mu	Omega Mu	a fictious clan of overweight people	S
perma-fried	perma-fried	to appear as if on drugs, even though one is sober	S

shoot the breeze	to chat				
	shoot the breeze	S	whodi	friend	
talk to Ralph on the big white telephone	to vomit			whodi	S
	talk to Ralph on the….	S	wife-beater	a sleeveless undershirt	
USer	a resident or citizen of the United States			wife-beater	S
	USer	S	yada	et cetera	
What's the dilly?	a greeting			yada	S
	What's the dilly?	S	za	abbreviation of "pizza"	
				za	S

archetype	an original model or pattern from which other later copies are made	archetype	L
antithesis	using opposite phrases in one breath	antithesis	L
asterisk	this symbol *	asterisk	L
bilabial	sounds that need the lower and upper lip to be made	bilabial	L
Byronic hero	antihero who is a romanticized but wicked character	Byronic hero	L
cacophony	sharp and hissing sounds	cacophony	L
chain of being	cosmological model of the universe	chain of being	L
chronicle	history of events	chronicle	L

climax	point of greatest intensity		couplet	two lines of text	
	climax	L		couplet	L
colloquialism	words used in everyday speech but seldom in written language		cyrillic	alphabet used to write in Russia	
	colloquialism	L		cyrillic	L
connotation	emotional resonance a word carries along its original meaning		denotation	exact meaning of the word	
	connotation	L		denotation	L
cothurni	Greek word for the shoes actors wore		denouement	final outcome of a story	
	cothurni	L		denouement	L

dactyl	dactyl	a 3 syllable metric foot
decorum	decorum	the necessity that a character was matched in his actions, character etc
deism	deism	rational approach to understand god in literature
deus ex machina	deus ex machina	an unrealistic and unexpected intervention
deuteronomic law	deuteronomic law	belief that god could wait with his punishment for some generations
ding dong theory	ding dong theory	linguistic theory that language began as an reaction to external stimulation
ellipsis	ellipsis	leaving out words
verbal ejaculation	verbal ejaculation	interjection expressing strong emotions

encyclical	official written note of the pope	
	encyclical	L
enjambement	line having no punctuation at the end and continues over the next line	
	enjambement	L
epanalepsis	the same word at the beginning and end of a phrase	
	epanalepsis	L
epiphany	manifestation of God's presence in the world	
	epiphany	L

eschatology	philosophical branch focusing on the end of time	
	eschatology	L
etymology	the study of the origin of a word	
	etymology	L
etymon	an older word that is the source for a newer one	
	etymon	L
flashback	reference to any earlier event or prior to its beginning	
	flashback	L

foil	character that contrasts to highlight or emphasize opposing traits in another character	foil ⌐
forestage	part of the stage closest to the viewing audience.	forestage ⌐
Haiku	poetic form popular in Japan.	Haiku ⌐
henotheist	the worship of one god without denying the existence of other gods	henotheist ⌐
hyperbole	exaggeration or overstatement	hyperbole ⌐
hypocrites	the classical Athenian word for an actor	hypocrites ⌐
Idola	false images of the mind	Idola ⌐
Imprimatur	official license/permission to print or publish	Imprimatur ⌐

in medias res	classical tradition of starting in the middle of a narration	in medias res ⌐L
juxtaposition	the arrangement of two or more ideas in order to contrast / compare	juxtaposition ⌐L
lai	short narrative or lyrical poem intended to be sung	lai ⌐L
majuscule	large letter or a capital letter	majuscule ⌐L
maquama	Arabic stories in rhymed prose	maquama ⌐L
marginalia	Drawings, notations appearing in the margins of a medieval text	marginalia ⌐L
meme	an idea or pattern of thought	meme ⌐L
metafiction	fiction in which the subject of the story is the art of storytelling itself	metafiction ⌐L

metaliterature	literary art focused on the subject of literary art itself	metaliterature / L	onomastic	related to names	onomastic / L
mosaic authorship	medieval belief that Moses wrote all five books in the bible himself	mosaic authorship / L	oxymoron	using contradiction in a manner that oddly makes sense on a deeper level	oxymoron / L
OED	standard abbreviation among scholars for The Oxford English Dictionary	OED / L	palindrome	word, sentence, or verse that reads the same way backward or forward	palindrome / L
ollamh	an ancient Irish storyteller	ollamh / L	paralanguage	non-verbal features that accompany speech	paralanguage / L

peripeteia	the sudden reversal of fortune in a story, play or narrative	peripeteia ⌐
picaresque novel	an often autobiographical novel about a rogue or picaro (a person of low social status)	picaresque novel ⌐
sarcasm	another term for verbal irony	sarcasm ⌐
simile	an analogy or comparison	simile ⌐
stereotype	an ordinary or unoriginal character	stereotype ⌐
succubus	a demon-lover in feminine shape	succubus ⌐
incubus	a demon-lover in masculine shape	incubus ⌐
symploce	repeating words at both the beginning and the ending of a phrase	symploce ⌐

tabula rasa	tabula rasa — (erased table) the idea that humanity is born completely innocent	**weltansicht**	weltansicht — the general attitude towards life and reality an individual or character demonstrates
temporal	temporal — something relating to the element of time	**ubi sunt motif**	ubi sunt motif — a literal motif
vegetationsdämon	vegetationsdämon — spirit in mythology that represents the vitality of the native vegetation		
vocabulary	vocabulary — the stock of available words in a given language		

xenia

xenia | the greek term for the laws of hospitality | L

xenophanic

xenophanic | refers to wandering poets who make use of satire and witticism | L

weak ending

Weak ending | in poetry another term for a feminine ending in which the last syllable of a metrical line is unstressed | L

virelay

virelay | an old French term for a short poem consisting of short lines using two rhymes and two opening lines | L

weltschmerz

weltschmerz | sentimental pessimism expressing sorrow, | L

variorum

variorum | version of an author's work containing notes and comments. | L

versification

versification | the making of verse | L

volta

volta | a volta is a sudden change in thought, direction or emotion near the conclusion of a sonnet | L

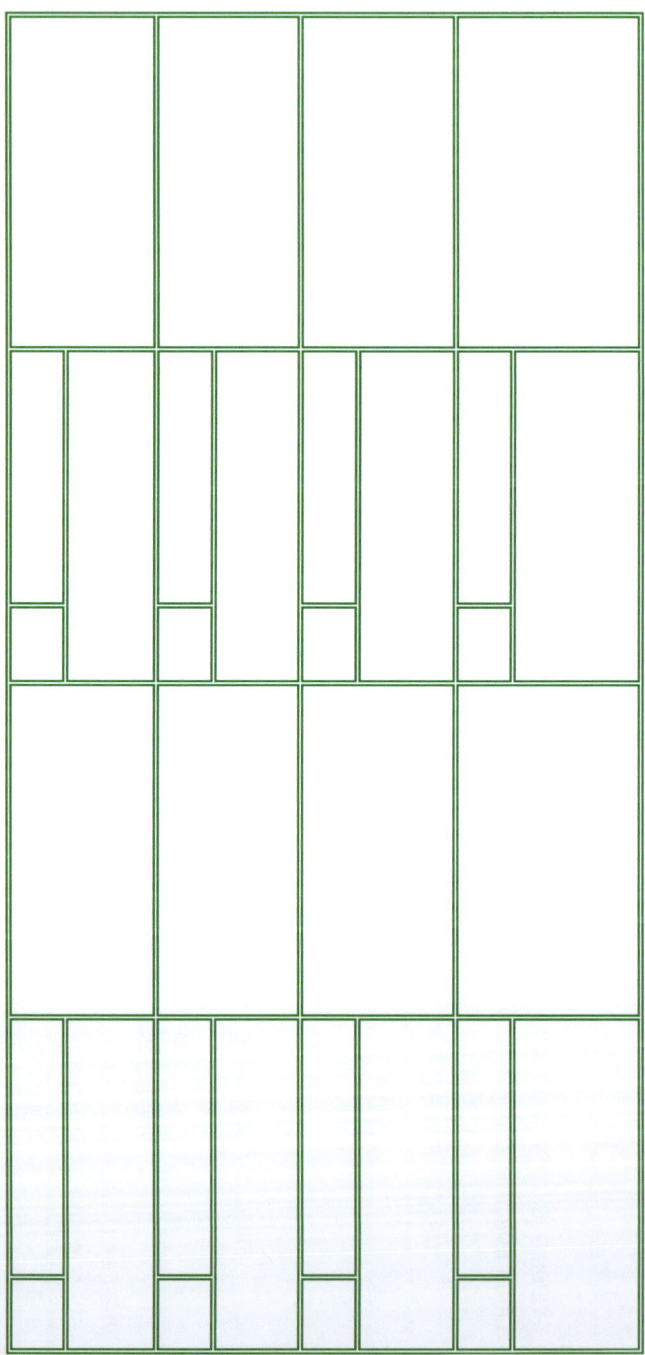

Zoloft	an antidepressant drug	
	Zoloft	M
ZOE	zinc oxide and eugenol	
	ZOE	M
zirconium	chemical element nr. 40	
	zirconium	M
zigadine	a plant toxin	
	zigadine	M

zooglea	a gelatinous mass	
	zooglea	M
zeony	the offspring of a zebra and a pony	
	zeony	M
zein	the main protein in maize	
	zein	M
zebronkey	cross between a zebra and a donkey	
	zebronkey	M

zafirlukast	an anti asthma drug	M
	zafirlukast	
Zalophus	a sealion	M
	Zalophus	
z-line	a dark thin protein band	M
	z-line	
xanthic	yellow	M
	xanthic	
woven bone	bony tissue characteristic of the embryonic skeleton	M
	woven bone	
wolf tooth	an extra tooth which can appear in the jaws of horses	M
	wolf tooth	
wistaria	a genus of climbing plants	M
	wistaria	
wohlfahrtiosis	infection caused by larvae of flies of the genus Wohlfahrtia	M
	wohlfahrtiosis	

word salad	mix of meaningless words emitted by persons with certain kinds of schizophrenia		wassail	an ancient expression of good wishes on a festive occasion	
	word salad	M		wassail	M
westness	the state of being wet		windburn	a reddened irritation of the skin caused by exposure to the wind	
	westness	M		windburn	M
wnl	within normal limits		webfoot	a foot with webbed toes	
	wnl	M		webfoot	M
water star grass	an aquatic plant		hydrocephalus	water on the brain	
	water star grass	M		hydrocephalus	M

Term	Definition	M
walleye	absence of color in the iris	
	walleye	M
wallaby	kangaroo-like creatures of small size	
	wallaby	M
vulpes vulpes	the red fox	
	vulpes vulpes	M
vox	voice	
	vox	M
vesication	visible accumulations of fluid within or beneath the epidermis	
	vesication	M
uberrimae fidei	the utmost good faith	
	uberrimae fidei	M
ulcer	local defect of the surface of an organ or tissue	
	ulcer	M
urodela	An order of the Amphibia class which includes salamanders and newts	
	urodela	M

takifugu	takifugu	a genus of pufferfish commonly used for research	M
tibias	tibias	the second longest bone of the skeleton	M
tabanid	tabanid	bloodsucking flies of the family Tabanidae	M
serendipity	serendipity	happy finding of an unexpected object or solution while searching for something else	M

superego	superego	component of the personality - the "conscience"	M
sutures	suture	materials used in closing a surgical wound	M
radarkymography	radarkymography	Video tracking of heart motion	M
radiable	radiable	capable of being penetrated or examined by rays, especially x-rays	M

rutabaga	A plant species of the family CRUCIFERAE best known for the edible roots	
	rutabaga	M
quackery	the fraudulent misrepresentation of the diagnosis and treatment of disease	
	quackery	M
palates	the structure that forms the roof of the mouth	
	palates	M
previus	of or relating to the blockage of passages in childbirth	
	previus	M
potaba	A member of the VITAMIN B COMPLEX	
	potaba	M
omnipen	Semi-synthetic derivative of penicillin that functions as an orally active broad-spectrum antibiotic	
	omnipen	M
orofacial	relating to the mouth and face	
	orofacial	M
otalgia	pain in the ear	
	otalgia	M

nobelium	A man-made radioactive element . Number 102	
	nobelium	M
nucleus ruber	a pinkish-yellow portion of the midbrain	
	nucleus ruber	M
nature	the system of all phenomena in space and time; the totality of physical reality	
	nature	M
matrix unguis	nail bed	
	matrix unguis	M
morula	the early embryo at the developmental stage	
	morula	M
meteorology	the atmospheric events which relate to climate and weather	
	meteorology	M
latebra	part of a bird's egg	
	latebra	M
laser knife	use of a laser to make bloodless cuts in tissue	
	laser knife	M

Latinas	latinas	M	Mexican Americans		
			jararaca	jararaca	M
				a kind of poisonous snakes	
Kanpo	Kanpo	M			
	System of herbal medicine practiced in Japan		**jugular veins**	jugular veins	M
				veins in the neck	
kahuna ana'ana	kahuna ana'ana	M	**Jupiter**	Jupiter	M
	Hawaiian culture, black magician who can cast spells to bring about death to a person			The fifth planet in order from the sun	
kaolin	kaolin	M	**iguana**	iguana	M
	fine white clay used to make porcelain			large herbivorous tropical American lizards	

insomnias	disorders characterized by impairment of the ability to initiate or maintain sleep		guanaco	a mammals of South America, they are related to camels	
	insomnias	M		guanaco	M
iatric	of or relating to medicine or a physician		geophagy	the eating of earthy substances, such as clay or chalk	
	iatric	M		geophagy	M
habu	snakes of the family of viperidae		Gore Tex	a nonflammable, tough, plastic material used in clothes	
	habu	M		Gore Tex	M
huffing	breathing in glue or hair spray		frons	forehead	
	huffing	M		forehead	M

frostbite	injury to tissues due to exposure to cold	
	frostbite	M
flatus	production or presence of gas in the gastrointestinal tract which may be expelled through the anus	
	flatus	M
efavirenz	a drug used to treat HIV infection	
	efavirenz	M
effemination	the acquisition of feminine characteristics	
	effemination	M
embolism	blocking of a blood vessel by a blood clot	
	embolism	M
detoxify	to remove the effects of poison from something, such as the blood	
	detoxify	M
devata	the process of gaining knowledge or a deity	
	devata	M
donkeys	family of hoofed mammals like asses, horses and zebras.	
	donkeys	M

Term	Definition	M
cranial	toward the head end of the body	
	cranial	M
cobalt	a trace element that is a component of vitamin B12	
	cobalt	M
clubfoot	a deformed foot	
	clubfoot	M
Beauceron	a large French sheepdog	
	Beauceron	M

Term	Definition	M
Bufo	the family of true toads	
	Bufo	M
biofilm	films (layers) of bacteria or other microbial organisms	
	biofilm	M
analergine	an antagonist of histamine H1 receptors	
	analergine	M
anility	the state of existing as or like an old woman	
	anility	M

acronychal	acronychal	W	rising at nightfall
albertopolis	albertopolis	W	cultural sites in South Kensington, London
adipocere	adipocere	W	waxy fat of a dead person
anatine	anatine	W	duck-like
antimacassar	antimacassar	W	clothing for the back of a chair
astrobleme	astrobleme	W	old meteor impact crater
balafon	balafon	W	an African music instrument
boondoggle	boondoggle	W	do useless work

abiturient	abiturient	W
	pupil leaving school	
abolla	abolla	W
	roman military cloak	
abra	abra	W
	narrow mountain pass	
acaudate	acaudate	W
	tailless	

arboriform	arboriform	W
	shaped like a tree	
aquifer	aquifer	W
	rock formation containing water	
arachnivorous	arachnivorous	W
	eating spiders	
archididascalos	archididascalos	W
	headmaster of a school	

arctophile	collector of teddy bears		**cruciverbalist**	a compiler or solver of crossword puzzles	
	arctophile	W		cruciverbalist	W
Brimborion	a thing without value or use		**deasil**	righthandwards; clockwise, in the direction of the sun	
	Brimborion	W		deasil	W
cacography	bad handwriting		**discombobulate**	to confuse	
	cacography	W		discombobulate	W
confute	prove to be wrong		**dumbledore**	a type of bee	
	confute	W		dumbledore	W

Word	Definition	W
deray	tumult, confusion	
	deray	W
ergophobia	fear of work	
	ergophobia	W
eyot	a small island	
	eyot	W
esculent	edible, fit to be eaten	
	esculent	W
epeolatry	literally: the worship of words	
	epeolatry	W
ensorcelled	enchanted, bewitched	
	ensorcelled	W
flabbergasted	surprised	
	flabbergasted	W
fletcherise	to chew thoroughly	
	fletcherise	W

Word	Definition		W
floccinauci-nihilipilification	habit of judging someone worthless	floccinauci-nihilipilification	W
frigorific	causing cold, chilling	frigorific	W
figurate	metaphorical	figurate	W
gabelle	a tax on salt	gabelle	W
gazebo	small building in a garden with a good view	gazebo	W
gurning	pulling grotesque faces	gurning	W
gomer	undesirable hospital patient	gomer	W
Garmagon	a mythical beast	Gormagon	W

haggard	looking exhausted, unwell
ha-ha	a boundary to a park or garden that doesn't interrupt the view.
hodening	masquerade on Christmas Eve in Kent.
honeyfuggle	to deceive or obtain sth.. by cheating
humicubation	the act of lying on the ground
ice house	a building used to preserve winter ice for use in summer
inwit	conscience ; wisdom
inglenook	a chimney corner

interrobang	a combined exclamation mark and question mark	
	interrobang	W
incunabulum	a book printed before 1501	
	incunabulum	W
in silico	in or by means of a computer simulation	
	in silico	W
isabelline	af yellow – greyish colour	
	isabelline	W
jackalope	a mythical horned rabbit	
	jackalope	W
jackanapes	a cheeky or impertinent person	
	jackanapes	W
jaculation	the act of throwing	
	jaculation	W
jingoism	aggressive or warlike patriotism	
	jingoism	W

Word	Definition	W
katzenjammer	a hangover katzenjammer	W
kinetoscope	an early motion picture device kinetoscope	W
knucker	a water demon knucker	W
lackadaisical	lacking enthusiasmus and interest lackadaisical	W

Word	Definition	W
latrociny	robbery; brigandage latrociny	W
leechcraft	the art of healing	W
lycantrophy	the supposed transformaton into a werewolf lycantrophy	W
lollygag	to fool around lollygag	W

Word	Definition		W
lithophone	a percussion instrument made of stone	lithophone	W
macaronic	a verse made up of mixed languages	macaronic	W
lollapaloosa	something exceptionally good of its kind	lollapaloosa	W
mundungus	rubbish;refuse	mundungus	W
magiric	relating to cooking	magiric	W
mudlark	someone who scavenges in river mud for items of value	mudlark	W
musterdevillers	a type of mixed grey woollen cloth	musterdevillers	W
mortsafe	an iron frame put over a coffin to prevent the body being stolen	mortsafe	W

Word	Definition	W
metemptosis	omission of the extra day of a leap year	W
nepenthes	a drug or potion bringing welcome forgetfulness	W
nepenthes	nepenthes	W
nescient	ignorant	W
nescient	nescient	W
nihilartikel	a fake entry in a dictionary	W
nihilartikel	nihilartikel	W

Word	Definition	W
ninnyhammer	a fool	
ninnyhammer	ninnyhammer	W
nipperkin	an old unit of volume	W
nipperkin	nipperkin	W
nut-crack night	Halloween	W
nut-crack night	nut-crack night	W
nychthemeron	a period of a day and night, 24 hours	W
nychthemeron	nychthemeron	W

obnubilate	to reduce visibility, to darken obnubilate	W
oche	the line behind which darts players stand when throwing oche	W
octothorpe	another name for the telephone handset symbol # octothorpe	W
olitory	relating to vegetables or the kitchen garden olitory	W
omnium-gatherum	a miscellaneous collection omnium-gatherum	W
omphaloskepsis	use the own navel to meditate omphaloskepsis	W
onomasticon	collection of names / words , a dictionary onomasticon	W
onychophagist	a person who bites his or her nails onychophagist	W

orismology	the science of defining technical terms	
	orismology	W
oxter	the armpit	
	oxter	W
palimpsest	a parchment which has been erased and rewritten	
	palimpsest	W
pantechnicon	a furniture removal van	
	pantechnicon	W

pyknic	short and fat	
	pyknic	W
picadil	an applied shape on the edge of clothing, especially a collar	
.		W
POTUS	President of the United States	
	POTUS	W
pogonotrophy	beard-growing	
	pogonotrophy	W

Word	Definition		W
pulchritudinous	beautiful	pulchritudinous	W
piepowder	a ravelling man or trader	piepowder	W
portolan	book containing charts and sailing directions	portolan	W
petrichor	the smell of rain on dry ground.	petrichor	W
quocker-wodger	a wooden puppet on a string	quocker-wodger	W
rantipole	a wild or bad behaving young person	rantipole	W
roo	to pluck the wool from the fleece of a sheep	roo	W
robinsonade	A novel with a theme similar to that of Robinson Crusoe	robinsonade	W

rasorial	rasorial — scratching the ground for food (usually done by chicken etc.)	W
rhinotillexomania	rhinotillexomania — habitual or obsessive nose-picking	W
sabermetrician	sabermetrician — someone who fervently analyzes baseball statistics	W
subfusc	subfusc — dull ; dark; gloomy	W
sphairistike	sphairistike — a ball game that developed into tennis	W
steganography	steganography — the art of creating and transmitting hidden messages	W
smellfeast	smellfeast — a parasite, a greedy sponger,	W
spanghew	spanghew — to throw into the air	W

Word	Definition	W
sennight	a week	
	sennight	W
spondulicks	money, cash	
	spondulicks	W
simoleon	one dollar	
	simoleon	W
stultiloquy	foolish babbling	
	stultiloquy	W

Word	Definition	W
stillicide	a falling of water in drops	
	stillicide	W
tatterdemalion	a tattered or ragged person	
	tatterdemalion	W
teetotum	a small spinning top	
	teetotum	W
thelemic	permitting people to do as they like	
	thelemic	W

therianthrope	a being that is part animal, part human		triskaidekaphobia	fear of the number 13	
	therianthropoe	W		triskaidekaphobia	W
tiffin	lunch, or any light meal		tintinnabulation	a ringing or tinkling sound	
	tiffin	W		tintinnabulation	W
trebuchet	a medieval military siege engine for hurling heavy missiles		ultimo	relating to last month	
	trebuchet	W		ultimo	W
titubation	a staggering or unsteadiness of walk or posture		ultracrepidarian	somebody who gives opinions on matters beyond his knowledge	
	titubation	W		ultracrepidarian	W

unobtanium	a material that is unobtainable, often because it doesn't exist	
	unobtanium	W
ullage	the unfilled space in a barrel or wine bottle	
	ullage	W
vaccary	a cow pasture	
	vaccary	W
vaccimulgence	the milking of cows	
	vaccimulgence	W

venery	hunting; the chase	
	venery	W
vexillology	the study of flags	
	vexillology	W
vinolent	addicted to wine; intemperate or drunken	
	vinolent	W
vomitorium	an opening in a Roman theatre	
	vomitorium	W

Term	Definition	Guess 1		Guess 2	
volitation	flying, flight	volitation	W		
wobbegong	an Australian shark	wobbegong	W		
welkin	the sky; heaven; the firmament	welkin	W		
whilom	an adjective meaning former	whilom	W		

Term	Definition	Guess 1	
xenoglossy	the ability to speak a language without having learned it	xenoglossy	W
yuletide	christmas	yuletide	W
zenzizenzizenzic	the eigth power of a number	zenzizenzizenzic	W
zany	amusingly crazy or clownish	zany	W

Last words

Herstellung und Verlag:
Books on Demand GmbH, Norderstedt
ISBN 978-3-8391-2555-7

I personally thank Walter Rader of The Online Slang Dictionary (http://onlineslangdictionary.com/) for contributing some definitions and the helpful exchange.

Would you like to comment or contribute some fresh words ? Feel free to write to: Creativity@gmx.biz

This is version 2.4.